THE ROAD THAT LEADS

TO FREEDOM

FINISHING STRONG!

TERESA A. STITH

The Road That Leads to Freedom

Copyright © 2021 Teresa A. Stith

Unless otherwise identified, scripture quotations are from the King James Version of the Bible. Copyright © 1982 by Thomas Nelson, Inc. Used by permission. All rights reserved.

Please note that certain pronouns referring to the Father, Son, and Holy Spirit may be capitalized to acknowledge God and any such titles referring to Him. Please note just the opposite when referring to satan. We choose not to capitalize his name or acknowledge him in any way, even to the point of violating grammatical rules.

ISBN-13: 978-1-7332744-5-6

Publisher- A Faith That Works Publishing

Website: afaiththatworks.com

FINISH STRONG!

**FORGET
WHAT HURT YOU
BUT NEVER FORGET
WHAT YOU
LEARNED FROM IT!**

INTRODUCTION

Before you dive into the pages of this book, it is my hope that you will pray, meditate and earnestly give yourself to "hear" those long awaited answers to questions you may have had for much of your life. There's a reason why you still feel stuck. There's a reason why you're still here. It is my hope that I can help you to understand the "why?"

The road that leads to freedom is indeed a bumpy road. A road that is filled with many setbacks, hindrances, sadness, grief, etc. But it's also a road that is filled with happiness, joy, success, and accomplishments, depending on how you're able to maneuver its twists and turns. Sooo...imagine this: If you are driving along and see a bump or pothole in the middle of the road, you're not just going to run over top of it right? No, you're going to slow down and at least investigate the situation before proceeding to go any further. We have to approach life the same way. Sometimes it's needful to just slow down and investigate or consider the decisions and choices that we are making. Being hasty with our desires because of something that we want or think that we need right now may cause grave consequences later. This has been one of my strongest battles. Because I was a person who grew up struggling, whenever I did receive something good, I either squandered or misused it because I didn't know how to handle it. God wants you to be free, so in this season you must pay close attention to your inner ear. The need to discern motives is crucial in this season and I'm not just talking about other people's motives. I'm talking about yours too!

This book is a compilation of questions and thoughts derived from the late Dr. Miranda T. Ruffin, geared toward helping you to be free from past hurts, bitterness, unforgiveness, or whatever has been holding you back and preventing you from stepping fully into experiencing true "freedom in Christ". You picked up this book because YOU KNOW that there is something in you pulling you toward this freedom. You've gotten the scrapes and bruises, you've made the tough decisions, now prepare yourself to DO what needs to be done to enjoy the rest of your life free from the cares and the toils that the world pushes upon you. You don't have to be miserable. YOU have the power to CHOOSE your path and own your own destiny. Let's take a look at what's trying to secretly hide away in your heart, let's address it, and let's MOVE YOU FORWARD!

DOES GOD HAVE YOUR ATTENTION NOW?

TABLE OF CONTENTS

"I have walked that long road to freedom. I have tried not to falter; I have made missteps along the way. But I have discovered the secret that after climbing a great hill, one only finds that there are many more hills to climb. I have taken a moment here to rest, to steal a view of the glorious vista that surrounds me, to look back on the distance I have come."

-Nelson Mandela

ARE YOU UNTEACHABLE?
1

How does a person become unteachable? You usually won't recognize it at first. As a matter of fact, it may take someone else to point it out for you. Well for me, God was the one who did the pointing it out. My First Lady (the Late Dr. Miranda T. Ruffin) was an amazing Bible scholar (as I would call her) who listened intently to the voice of God and lived a life of total obedience to Him. She could discern many things and operated in several of the gifts of the Spirit. There were many days and nights that I laid at her feet inquiring and just wanting to know more about what I could do to experience God like she could. She made it look so easy. She assured me that if I just let God have His way in my life, that He would give me what I was desiring of Him. Omg, I wanted it so bad and was even more excited to hear that I may actually have a chance at obtaining these Spiritual things that I had been seeking from the Lord.

One night (November 26, 2013 to be exact) the Lord laid it on First Lady's heart to make paper hearts for all of the women in our Women's Group and write one word on the heart that we would be able to readily identify with. The Lord obviously had already given her the word to write on each individual heart that she made. She turned them all face down, mixed them all up and one by one, we stepped forth to choose a heart and tell why we thought we got the word that we did. This went on for two weeks straight (we only met on Monday nights) and each night, both weeks, I got the same word. I thought "now how is this even possible?" The first time that I got the word "unteachable" it was really no big deal, "I thought" but the second time that I pulled the same card, it hit me a little differently, like God was really trying to get my attention concerning something that He was obviously concerned about in me, and that could possibly become a hindrance to where He was trying to take me. My heart was completely broken as I wondered "what was I doing wrong?" I tell you what, I left that meeting and I did not rest well that night. All I could think about was that the Lord had a problem with me and I needed to quiet myself before Him so that He could show me what I needed to do to fix it! The Lord did as promised. As I stilled myself before Him, He showed me some things about myself.

THE ROAD THAT LEADS TO FREEDOM

I HAD BECOME COMFORTABLE

I had become too comfortable where I was. Matter of fact, I had become so comfortable that I stopped reaching. I stopped trying, and I stopped seeking. I had become so comfortable with where I was that I had stopped to rest in a place that was far from where God was trying to take me and I wasn't listening to Him telling me that it was time for me to MOVE. I was resisting God by backing away when He was urging me to "go forth." I was doing what I wanted to do and had not realized that I had become "settled" or "unteachable" meaning that I was closing my ears to anything else (anything new) that was trying to get in. This is a very dangerous place to be Spiritually as the enemy tries to feed you thoughts that if you're not fully aware of his strategy, will have you turning back to the world and somewhere wondering how you got back there. There were other women in the group that because they were Teachers, they held a special place over us who were being taught. This is why I had received the word "unteachable" twice because I thought that I knew just as much as them and that I did not have to listen. Boy, if the Lord did not deal with me!

What the Lord showed me was that in Philippians 2:5, Jesus Christ was humble, willing to give up His rights in order to obey God and serve people. Like Christ, we should have a servant's attitude, serving out of love for God and for others and not out of guilt or fear. We can choose our attitudes. We can approach life expecting to be served, or look for opportunities to serve others.

THE ROAD THAT LEADS TO FREEDOM

What have you learned from hearing, listening and obeying God's voice? Have you been listening, hearing, and obeying God's voice? Why? Why not?

_____

_____

_____

_____

_____

_____

_____

_____

_____

_____

_____

_____

_____

_____

_____

_____

Consider acknowledging God in all of your ways. Form a habit of just calling on Him and asking Him to show you what to do. Seek His help continuously throughout life's journey and trust in His ability to provide what you need to survive and sustain yourself. God's way is a way of peace and you will find peace every time that you include God in your day to day affairs.

Believe God. Yearn for Him through prayer. Your yearning to pray should stem from your desire for Him. It is an honor to be in the presence of the Lord so let us examine ourselves thoroughly before we even approach Him. This allows us to respect His presence and understand that we are standing on holy ground before a holy God, and that should be taken seriously.

THE ROAD THAT LEADS TO FREEDOM

I have learned to do "what" when I pray?

_____

_____

_____

_____

_____

_____

_____

_____

_____

_____

_____

_____

_____

_____

_____

_____

_____

_____

_____

_____

_____

_____

_____

_____

_____

CHILDHOOD EXPERIENCES

2

What are some things that you now understand about your childhood that kept you walking in your own thinking, decisions, etc?

_____

_____

_____

_____

_____

_____

_____

_____

_____

_____

_____

_____

_____

_____

_____

_____

_____

THE ROAD THAT LEADS TO FREEDOM

We experienced a lot of things in our childhood years, much of what we could not control as children. We grew up with differences of opinions about things, biases toward other people and how they behave, and we adapted to certain lifestyles all because of what we saw as children or what we were taught as a result of someone else's behavior. It's sad to say but much of that stuff grew up with us as we grew into adults, and now seeds of bitterness, envy, and strife is a result of not reaching out for help sooner because of who we thought we would hurt or who may be upset with us for sharing our story. To a certain extent, I controlled my childhood. My parents separated and divorced when I was very young and at a young age, I found myself providing for myself and making decisions for myself. Because I was given so much control at an early age, it was hard to break that mentality when I got older. I wanted to control everything. It put strains on my relationships with people and even on my success in life because of the strong will that I had developed that it was going to be "my way" or the highway. Well, it was certainly the highway for a lot of people and I think that they were glad to get away from around me because I couldn't see things from their point of view because I was so strong in what I believed whether it was right or wrong. Please don't let this be YOU! I'm so glad to have had God in my life at this time because I truly would have been living this life by myself with no friends, no help, no one to comfort or advise me because I was so set in my ways. It was only when God said to me "deny yourself" that I awoke out of this sleep and began to listen

intently to what He was saying to me about
"me." Also by this time, I had already started
the cycle of having children without their
fathers being present in their lives and I see
that many of the decisions that I made from
places of pain are now rearing their ugly heads
in my children's lives. We call them
generational curses, but they have to STOP
somewhere! I pray that whatever your
childhood experience may have been, that you
are able to shut the door on some things so that
your children or grandchildren would not have
to continue fighting battles that we should
have killed at the root! So then what are we
willing to change about our story so that our
children can be free? Or do we still want to be
justified in holding on to grief or pain as a
result of some kind of abuse? I'm not saying
that the abuse is justified, but I am saying that

we cannot stay in that place. We have to be
willing to cast that care on Jesus. There is
nothing that we can physically do to change
the outcome of what happened to us, it
happened. But God gives us the grace to be
able to move forward in it, IF we want to.
Notice that I said "we" because yes, I too, am a
victim of childhood abuse in some form. But it
DID NOT prevent the outcome of my story
from being great. As a matter of fact, it helped
it to be GREATER as I was able to share my
story to help other people. Look at God! God's
wisdom has not only taught me how to be
open to other people's views, but also how to
rightly divide the Word of truth.

I have changed this one thing about myself

_____
_____
_____
_____
_____

THE ROAD THAT LEADS TO FREEDOM

_____

_____

_____

_____

_____

_____

_____

My Favorite Scripture Is... why?

_____

_____

_____

_____

_____

_____

_____

_____

_____

_____

_____

_____

_____

_____

_____

_____

WHAT'S THE TRUTH?

3

There may be a lot of facts about things that have happened in your life, but the TRUTH is that you don't have to live with the facts when the truth is far greater. The Bible tells us in John chapter 8:36 that "if the Son therefore shall make you free, ye shall be free indeed. Simply meaning that God's truth outweighs the facts. You may be able to argue a fact, but the TRUTH will stand forever! You can't bend it, you can't break it, it holds its own. It STANDS SURE!

I have learned this one thing about truth

_____
_____
_____
_____
_____
_____

THE ROAD THAT LEADS TO FREEDOM

_____
_____
_____
_____
_____
_____
_____
_____
_____
_____

There were things that happened in my life that I wanted to feel justified about feeling some kind of way about them, but every time I went to the Word of God about it, I got the same response over and over again. That God had freed me from it and I should not ever entertain walking in it again. Why do we want to hold so tight on to something that God is trying to free us from? What purpose is it fulfilling in our lives? Who is being healed by you holding on to it? The people who may have hurt you have probably gone on with their lives and to you seems to be rather enjoying life, but here you are still stuck because of some hurt that you were never able to overcome. Listen, I'm not saying that you should not grieve. I'm not saying that you should be numb to any traumatic experience, but I am saying that you need to channel that energy into something positive that is going to heal that other person that may have that experience. It should not take you years to heal when the truth that is found in God's word is ALIVE and ACTIVE in us! Talk about it, testify about it. Help yourself to heal by sharing your experience and how it helped to shape you into the person you are today. This book is talking about "the road to freedom" and to travel this and actually come to a place of freedom rests upon you taking the steps that you need to take to overcome bad and/or past experiences.

THE ROAD THAT LEADS TO FREEDOM

It's all because of this emotion or feeling

_____

_____

_____

_____

_____

_____

_____

_____

_____

_____

_____

_____

_____

_____

_____

_____

_____

_____

Listen, feelings change. What is the truth about why you feel the way that you feel? Because God cuts things at the root. He deals with truth. In order to come to a place of freedom, you have to be honest with yourself.

Stop turning a deaf ear or a blind eye to things that need to be addressed. Address it! Stop playing with the devil while he continues to wreak havoc in your life. Don't give him any more control or access to your future by holding you to your past. Let it go!

Despite all of the negative and incomplete things that have fallen to waste in your life, the insecurities, and the weight of guilt and shame, stay motivated to push onward. Realize that there are others out here watching and waiting for you to pull through because they need to know how you did it. You may be their motivation to fight through what they're dealing with. Don't give up. You are helping someone else to have hope so DO NOT QUIT!

THE ROAD THAT LEADS TO FREEDOM

What is the motto about your change?

_____

_____

_____

_____

_____

_____

_____

_____

_____

_____

My motto has been "you are what you eat." This helps me to realize that I am ultimately in control of what I allow into my life, my heart, my mind, my Spirit, my house, etc. You too, are in control of and have power over your thoughts and emotions. Don't be robbed of the keys that you hold to the truths in your life that outweighs the facts that may be present.

T. A. STITH

Lord help me to understand why I am still battling with: (May have more than one)

{bitterness   {spending money   {selfishness

{secret thoughts   {disobedience   {overeating

{lust   {hatred   {fear   {anger

{other:_____

_____

_____

_____

_____

_____

_____

_____

_____

_____

_____

_____

_____

_____

_____

_____

_____

_____

_____

_____

_____

THE ROAD THAT LEADS TO FREEDOM

I have always felt that I needed to defend myself. Sure, I had a very dark past and was very promiscuous at one point in my life simply because I was looking for love not really understanding what that was in my young years. I thought that it was good sex. Unbeknownst to me, it was far from that. Once I gave my life to the Lord and began to change my ways and clean up my life, I still found myself trying to defend myself to people who didn't believe in the work that God had done on the inside to completely transform my life. There are still a few devils out here that tries every now and again to sneak that "remember when" game on me and I have to pull out my sword and go to battle. God does not hold your past against you, so don't let people make you feel some kind of way about yours either. Keep moving forward toward your freedom!

I have now committed/accepted this about my life

_____
_____
_____
_____
_____
_____
_____
_____
_____
_____
_____
_____
_____
_____
_____
_____
_____
_____
_____
_____
_____
_____
_____
_____
_____
_____
_____
_____
_____
_____

THE ROAD THAT LEADS TO FREEDOM

Now when I look at my children/family, I see:

_____
_____
_____
_____
_____
_____
_____
_____
_____
_____
_____
_____

With them I have learned

_____
_____
_____
_____
_____
_____
_____
_____
_____
_____
_____
_____

I have given up these things about my own desires for God

_____

_____

_____

_____

_____

_____

_____

_____

_____

_____

_____

_____

_____

_____

_____

_____

We desire all of these things from God, but what are we willing to sacrifice and give up that He can become more real to us? In Mark 8:34 Jesus called the people and His followers to Him and said "if anyone wants to be My follower, he must give up himself and his own desires. He must take up his cross and follow Me." How does this make you feel that God would ask you to give up something that may be of value to you? Is this why you cannot follow Him wholeheartedly because of something that you wish to hold on to? Someone? Be honest. The road to freedom forces you to take a close look at these things and to know your own heart concerning them. Romans 1:24 (paraphrasing) the people had become so vile against the ordinances of God and wanted so badly what they desired that God gave them up to their own dishonorable passions that even the women exchanged natural relations for unnatural ones. God will not save you if you do not want to be saved. He will not interfere with your choice. Know this though, that you will reap whatsoever you sow.

STOP THE MADNESS!

4

Please think before you answer this question (What are you doing right now that you have been warned about and still have not STOPPED THE MADNESS?!)

_____
_____
_____
_____
_____
_____
_____
_____
_____
_____
_____
_____
_____
_____
_____
_____
_____
_____

THE ROAD THAT LEADS TO FREEDOM

Listen, the road to freedom begins with you being honest with yourself about where you are and where you're trying to go. We have ALL sinned and fallen short of God's glory (Romans 3:23) so there is no need in being ashamed of where you are or the many times that you may have fallen trying to get this thing right. Yes, God knows our hearts, but He also wants to see an honest effort on your part to overcome this thing that has so easily beset you or hinders you. Why are you constantly falling down in it? What is it that you think that you need to stand up and walk this thing out? Is it just simply something that you do not want to let go? God wants to help you. Tell Him what you need to overcome this. How has your favorite scripture helped you in this area? How have you demonstrated your faith in the scripture you chose to sustain you?

I am still learning how to

_____
_____
_____
_____
_____
_____
_____
_____
_____
_____
_____
_____
_____

What has been a most significant change made in your life?

_____
_____
_____
_____
_____
_____
_____
_____
_____
_____

THE ROAD THAT LEADS TO FREEDOM

When I look at my life compared to that of others, I see...why is this important to me?

_____

_____

_____

_____

_____

_____

_____

_____

_____

_____

_____

When I envision where my life is going, I see

_____

_____

_____

_____

_____

_____

_____

_____

_____

Now this will take your honest opinion. Do not call names. Just say what's on your heart. **READ CAREFULLY AND ANSWER ALL QUESTIONS!**

When you look at those in your inner circle, you see...What is unique about them than any other person? Are you envious of them? Why? Why not?

_____
_____
_____
_____
_____
_____
_____
_____
_____
_____
_____
_____
_____
_____
_____
_____
_____
_____

THE ROAD THAT LEADS TO FREEDOM

Stop the madness! It's time for new thoughts, new ways of thinking, and a new outlook on life period! God is trying to get us to a place in life that when we go out amongst the world, that miracles, signs, and wonders will follow us. We need to get out of our feelings about things and get into our rightful places or we're going to miss the move of God in this season. You will not be able to prosper for God until you do.

Stop believing everything that folk say about you and learn how to walk in love. Learn to forgive and forgive people quickly. Unforgiveness in your heart will keep you from moving in the things of God. Remember to fast, pray, and stay humble. Keep loving people and above all else, DIE! We must learn to die from the ways of the world. Wherever we go and whatever we are ministering to people should leave a mark or identity that we are righteous, living people. When we go through our seasons of affliction, learn how to sing a song before the Lord. The devil hates that. But God loves it! We must stay on the path to our Heavenly calling and not become so overwhelmed with trying to please folk. Stay on assignment and let the blood of Jesus take care of that other stuff.

SOME OF US WANT THE BLESSINGS BUT WE DON'T WANT …

THE INSTRUCTIONS!

STOP THE MADNESS!

A Personal Relationship

5

What could a personal relationship with God mean to you? Let's analyze.

1. Stability
2. Substance
3. Resources
4. Fruit of the Spirit
5. Power
6. Free from distractions

Having a personal relationship with God means having the stability, the substance, and the resources available when life gets a little challenging. It means having those void places in your life filled. God teaches you how to interact with Him so that you also learn how to interact with others. The "fruits of the Spirit" helps us to understand what God is like and what He expects from us who bear His name

THE ROAD THAT LEADS TO FREEDOM

(Galatians 5:22-23).

There is so much going on in the world today and people are finding it difficult to cope with the pressures that life places upon them. Mental health is at an all-time high as people with no previous mental health issues are committing suicide and just "snapping out." It is important to have a relationship with God because He teaches you how to cast your cares upon Him (1 Peter 5:7). You have power over your thoughts and you retain that power by keeping your mind stayed on the Lord (Philippians 2:5).

Having a personal relationship with the Lord will help you to avoid the distractions that the enemy brings to keep us more focused on the world than on Jesus. We're so busy looking at how the wicked is prospering that we are forgetting that we have a mansion already prepared for us in Heaven. This is a season to not be so entangled with the world's affairs, but to incline our ears to hear what God is saying in this season. He wants a personal relationship with us. In Revelation 3:20, He says "Behold, I stand at the door, and knock: if any man hear my voice, and open the door, I will come in to him, and will sup with him, and he with Me. This is the only road that will lead to your freedom so let's FINISH STRONG!

> For the race is not given
> to the swift, nor to the strong,
> but to them that
> endures to the end
> -Ecclesiastes 9:11

"WHAT KIND OF

COMPETITOR

SEE'S THE

FINISH LINE

AND SLOWS DOWN

…ALWAYS

FINISH STRONG."

-Gary Ryan Blair

T. A. STITH

ABOUT THE AUTHOR

Born and raised in Brunswick County,
Virginia, Teresa found her love for writing in
her grade school years. She laughs as she
recalls how her Teachers would compliment
her handwriting being so young. She further
sharpened her skills as a writer through the
support of her English and Reading Teachers.
She loved school so much that she often found
herself playing school during the summer

months with her siblings and of course she was the "Teacher." Although, she never fully stepped into a teaching role, her wise counsel and the wisdom that she has shared with others have brought about tremendous changes in their lives. Her own personal battles drove her to find God at an early age and she has since found her calling in sharing those hard times with others and how her faith helped her to overcome the challenges of life. This is the sixth title in her collection of faith-based real life stories about her personal experiences that are sure to bring you victory over your own circumstances. Find this book and more at:

https://www.amazon.com/author/teresastith

Follow her on IG @afaiththatworks

Facebook @Afaiththatworks

Email: afaiththatworks@outlook.com

T. A. STITH

Visit her online store at:

https://www.faith-it-to-make-it.company.site

BE BLESSED!

CHECK OUT THESE NEW AND UPCOMING TITLES...

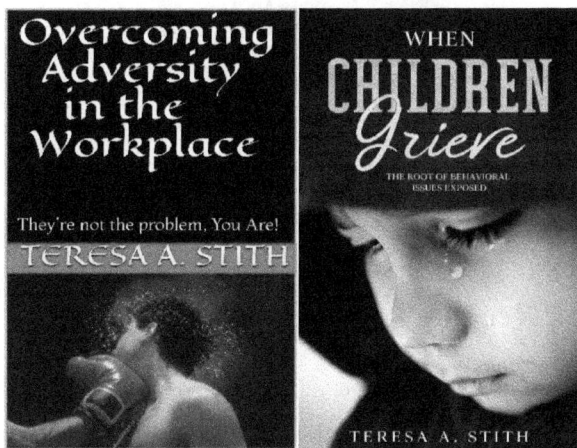

THE ROAD THAT LEADS TO FREEDOM

NEW AND UPCOMING TITLES

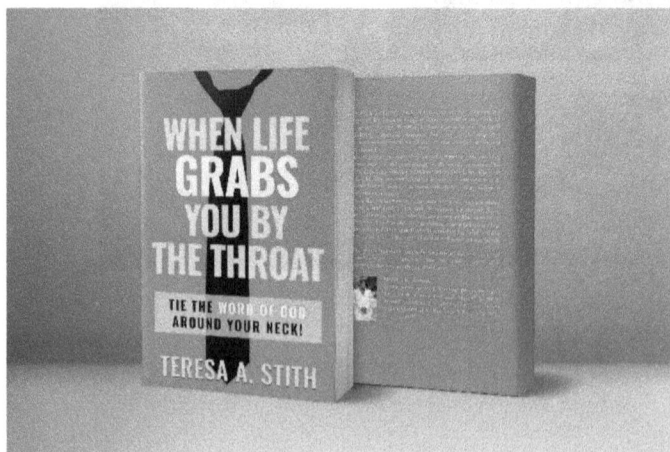

SOMETIMES THE WAY YOU

SEE THE PROBLEM...

IS THE PROBLEM

Be Free.

www.ingramcontent.com/pod-product-compliance
Lightning Source LLC
Chambersburg PA
CBHW051712090426
42736CB00013B/2657